Children's Dramas for the Church Year

Reproducible Dramas for Lent, Easter, and Pentecost

Abingdon Press
Nashville

ISBN 978-1-426-77865-0
PACP01358733-01

13 14 15 16 17 18 19 20 21 22—10 9 8 7 6 5 4 3 2 1

❧ Contents ❧

❧ Lent ❧

by Nancy Holbrook Sweeney

Christians know a special season
that leads them along the way.
Forty days of preparation,
to celebrate Easter Day.

Lent is a season when Christians
study the Bible and pray.
They pray for themselves and others
that God's will be done each day.

During Lent, Christians consider
how they live their lives each day.
They humbly pray, "God forgive us,
and help us to live your way."
Lent is a season when Christians
do things for those who have needs.
They share their belongings and skills
as Jesus taught by his deeds.

During Lent, Christians remember
Jesus—his life and his death.
They remember that God raised him.
He lives! Praise God with each breath!

✢ A Prayer for Shrove Tuesday ✢
by Peg Augustine

In the early church, people went to church to confess their sins on the day before Lent began on Ash Wednesday. Families gave up certain foods for Lent—eggs, meat, milk, and butter. On the Tuesday before Ash Wednesday, they had a feast to use up those foods. Today, churches often hold pancake suppers to celebrate the beginning of Lent. Use this prayer for Shrove Tuesday.

Dear God, as we eat this special meal tonight, help us to remember those who will be going to bed hungry. Bless those who have no place to sleep and no families to care for them.

Thank you for the food we eat every day and for those who prepare it for us. Thank you most of all for sending Jesus. Help us to remember him in a special way every day during Lent and to do the things he would have us do.

✢ Lent ✢
by Peg Augustine

Read Isaiah 2:3a, 5.

Come, let us walk in the light of the Lord that he may teach us his ways and that we may walk in his path.

> **L:** In the Lenten season, we remember Jesus is our Lord.
>
> **E:** Jesus came to earth for Everyone.
>
> **N:** Jesus told us, "Love your Neighbor."
>
> **T:** Thank you, God, for sending Jesus.

Sing, "Jesus, Remember Me" or "Jesus Loves Me."

Pray: Dear God, when all seems dark around us, help us to remember that Jesus brings us light. Amen.

A Pax Service

by Virginia Kessen

The word pax *is Latin for "peace." The pax service is a tenth-century English custom. The tradition reminded people who had quarreled or done wrong things during the past year that they could ask for and receive God's forgiveness.*

The leader begins the service by handing out two pretzels to each participant.

Leader: As you eat the first pretzel, think about the people you have quarreled with during the last year. Have you quarreled with a friend? a member of your family? someone at school? at church? *(Pause.)*

Forgive those people and forget those quarrels. Say a silent prayer for each person you have thought of.

Keep a few moments of silence while each person eats the first pretzel and prays in silence.

Leader: As you eat the second pretzel, think about the times during the past year when you have been thoughtless or cruel to someone.

Was it a brother or sister? a parent? someone who is unpopular at school? *(Pause.)*

Forgive your actions and remember that God forgives you.

Keep a few moments of silence while each person eats the second pretzel and prays in silence.

Leader: Amen. Now go from this place knowing that God is always ready to forgive us if we ask. Now go in peace!

✿ Symbols of Lent and Easter ✿

Production Notes

Encourage the children to make posters or to cut out pictures of the symbols to hold up as they speak. If you have a number of very young children who are too young for speeches, you might let them hold up the symbols while an older child or older children tell about the symbol.

Characters

Child 1	Child 2	Child 3
Child 4	Child 5	

Child 1: My symbol is the butterfly. The butterfly has become a symbol for Jesus' resurrection. A butterfly begins as an egg. Then it becomes a larvae, a caterpillar, a cocoon, and finally, a butterfly.

A butterfly totally changes from one kind of creature to another. When we love and follow Jesus, we change too.

Child 2: My symbol is a pretzel. It is usually associated with the forty days before Easter that we know as Lent. A tradition that began during those days was to eat bread shaped to look like little arms crossed in prayer. They called the bread *bracelae,* which means "little arms." In other parts of the world, people called it *bretzel,* which later became pretzel.

Now people eat pretzels all year long. The next time you are having a snack of pretzels, say a prayer for the people of the world who have no food.

Child 3: My symbol is new clothing. Many new believers were baptized at Easter. They were given new white robes to celebrate their new life in Christ.

Now people buy new clothing to wear on Easter morning to remind themselves that just as Jesus rose to new life, we have a new life when we give our hearts to Jesus.

Child 4: My symbol is spring flowers. Like the new clothes that people put on for Easter, the earth has beautiful new clothing each spring. As we look at the flowers, we remember that Jesus gave us new life too.

Child 5: My symbol is the Easter egg. During Lent, people in the early church did not eat eggs. But the chickens kept laying them anyway. So when Easter came, there were lots of eggs to use.

Kings gave specially decorated eggs to their subjects. People painted eggs and gave them to children. When you make and play with Easter eggs, remember that the greatest gift of all was Jesus.

Hosanna! Hosanna!
by Daphna Flegal

Hosanna! Hosanna! *(Wave palm branches.)*

It's Palm Sunday today. *(Brush palm branches on the floor.)*

We wave our palm branches *(Wave palm branches.)*

And happily say, *(Turn around.)*

"Hosanna! Hosanna!" *(Wave palm branches.)*

"Hosanna! Hosanna!" *(Wave palm branches.)*

It's Palm Sunday today. *(Brush palm branches on the floor.)*

We hear stories of Jesus *(Wave palm branches.)*

And happily say, *(Turn around.)*

"Hosanna! Hosanna!" *(Wave palm branches around.)*

❧ The Two Parades ❧

by Nate Lee

Production Notes

Two Groups enter the stage from either side. Group One, the smaller group, enters from the left. Group Two enters from the right. Except for the words spoken by the leaders, all of the other lines can be divided into however many people want parts. They are just designated as Group and Leader here. It would probably be more visually interesting if most of the larger and older kids are in Group Two.

Characters

Leader One	Leader Two
Group One	Group Two

Leader Two: *(to his own group)* Hurry up! I hear the horns. You don't want to be late.

Leader One: *(to his own group)* Come on, guys!

Group One: Yeah, hurry! Let's go! I can't wait to see him.

Group Two: How many horses do you think he'll have this time? How many soldiers? I love those uniforms.

The two groups meet in the middle of the stage. They know each other. There may seem to be a bit of hostility, not as in two different gangs, but perhaps two different cliques.

Leader Two: *(to Group and Leader One)* What? You guys lost? The parade is that way!

Leader One: Not the parade we're going to.

Leader Two: What? You're not going to see Pontius Pilate enter the city of Jerusalem on the first day of Passover?

Group Two: What is the matter with you? Isn't that against the law? Yeah! You have to go!

Leader One: Ahh, we've seen the governor.

Group One: Yeah, we needed a change. This is a different kind of parade.

Leader Two: Oh, yeah? What kind of change?

Leader One: Haven't you heard? Jesus of Nazareth is coming down from the Mount of Olives!

Leader Two: I've heard of him. The prophet?

Leader One: You could call him that. Or you could call him the Son of Man.

Leader Two: Hey, that's blasphemy!

Leader One: I didn't call him that. I only said you could call him that.

Leader Two: So, this Son of Man—this Messiah of yours—I suppose he's got an army of his own.

Group One: Of course not! No way! How uncool!

Group Two: No soldiers at all?

Group One: Probably not.

Group Two: No horses? No shiny shields? No shiny helmets? No spears or swords?

Group One: Nope. No way. Of course not! Not a chance!

Leader One: Just Jesus of Nazareth. Riding in on a colt.

Group One: And lots of people shouting, "Hosanna!" And putting their coats down on the path. And palm branches, of course. And even more "Hosannas!"

Leader One: You don't get that with Pontius Pilate's parade.

Leader Two: No, you don't. Haven't I read something in the Scriptures about this? Was this foretold or something?

Leader One: So you have been doing your homework. Yes, it was foretold in Zechariah.

Leader Two: Jesus of Nazareth riding in on a colt. Sounds cool!

Group Two: What are you talking about? What about the horses? And the shiny shields? And the shiny helmets? And the spears and swords?

Leader Two: Look. You guys can go to Pontius Pilate's parade. I'm going with these guys to see Jesus.

Group Two: What? Are you out of your mind? Come on, dude!

Leader Two: I understand if you guys want to see all the shiny stuff. Me, I've seen it before. Who knows? This may be the chance of a lifetime!

About half of Group Two come with Leader Two.

Group Two: Yeah, you may be right. I could use a change of pace myself. Hey, it's not so far to walk. Sounds like it could be pretty cool.

The larger Group One now moves off and toward the direction they were going, leaving a smaller Group Two.

Group Two: Ha! Some leader! He just went off with that other group! He's going to miss everything! Yeah. The horses. And the shiny shields. And the shiny helmets and spears and swords.

Group Two pauses as they look at the large Group One disappearing, and then look the other way, and then look back at the large Group One.

Group Two: You know, I don't think the governor will miss us at his stupid parade. Not a bit. Seen one Pontius procession, seem 'em all.

Group Two: And he did say it could be the chance of a lifetime.

Group Two: *(calling after Group One)* Hey! Wait for us! Wait up! We're coming! Hey, I know where we can pick up some palm branches on the way.

❧ The One Who Comes In Peace ❧

by Rev. Steve Richards and Linda Ray Miller

All selections are from the Good News Translation.

Characters

Prophet	Narrator

Everyone: Give thanks to the Lord, because he is good, and his love is eternal. Let the people of Israel say, "His love is eternal." Let the priests of God say, "His love is eternal." Let all who worship him say, "His love is eternal." In my distress I called to the Lord; he answered me and set me free. The Lord is with me, I will not be afraid. (Psalm 118:1-6)

Prophet: Rejoice, rejoice, people of Zion! Shout for joy, you people of Jerusalem! Look, your king is coming to you! He comes triumphant and victorious, but humble and riding on a donkey—on a colt, the foal of a donkey. (Zechariah 9:9)

Narrator: As [Jesus and his disciples] approached Jerusalem, near the towns of Bethphage and Bethany, they came to the Mount of Olives. Jesus sent two of his disciples on ahead with these instructions: "Go to the village there ahead of you. As soon as you get there, you will find a colt tied up that has never been ridden. Untie it and bring it here. And if someone asks you why you are doing that, tell him the Master needs it and will send it back at once." So they went and found a colt out in the street, tied to the door of a house. As they were untying it, some of the bystanders asked them, "What are you doing, untying that colt?" They answered just as Jesus had told them, and the crowd let them go. (Mark 11:1-6)

Prophet: Long ago, the people of Israel welcomed a new king. Here is how they welcomed him: Jehu said, "The prophet told me that the Lord proclaims: 'I anoint you king of Israel.'" At once Jehu's fellow officers spread their cloaks at the top of the steps for Jehu to stand on, blew trumpets, and shouted, "Jehu is king!" (2 Kings 9:12b-13, adapted)

Narrator: They [the disciples] brought the colt to Jesus, threw their cloaks over the animal, and Jesus got on. Many people spread their cloaks on the road, while others cut branches in the field and spread them on the road. The people who were in front and those who followed behind began to shout, "Praise God! God bless him who comes in the name of the Lord! God bless the coming kingdom of King David, our father! Praise be to God!" *(Mark 11:7-10)*

Everyone: The stone which the builders rejected as worthless turned out to be the most important of all. This was done by the Lord; what a wonderful sight it is! This is the day of the Lord's victory; let us be happy, let us celebrate! Save us, Lord, save us! Give us success, O Lord! May God bless the one who comes in the name of the Lord! From the Temple of the Lord we bless you. The Lord is God; he has been good to us. With branches in your hands, start the festival and march around the altar. *(Psalm 118:22-27)*

A Parade Is a Good Thing

by Gail Kittleson

This is such a special day:
Mother says Jesus is coming this way!
Grandma says, "Now, children, come along, come!"
In the distance, I hear a hum.
Father has spread his coat on the ground.
A donkey is coming—what is that sound?
People are shouting and cheering out loud.
What is the meaning of this big crowd?
Hosanna to him who comes in God's name,
Blessed is Jesus—the one who came.
They're worshiping him and singing psalms,
Shouting, laughing, and waving palms.
We know that this means he is the King;
That's the meaning of everything.

❧ Jesus Shared a Special Meal ❧

by Tim Edmonds

Sing to the tune of "Mary Had a Little Lamb."

Jesus shared a special meal, special meal, special meal.
Jesus shared a special meal so many years ago.

He passed around the juice and bread, juice and bread, juice and bread.
He passed around the juice and bread so many years ago.

We can share this special meal, special meal, special meal.
We can share this special meal with friends we've come to know.

❧ Jesus Loves His Friends ❧

by Daphna Flegal

Sing to the tune of "The Farmer in the Dell."
Jesus loved his friends. *(Circle right.)*

Jesus loved his friends. *(Circle left.)*

Hi-ho! I'm glad we know *(Move to the center.)*

That Jesus loved his friends. *(Move back out to the circle.)*

They shared a special meal. *(Circle right.)*

They shared a special meal. *(Circle left.)*

Hi-ho! I'm glad we know *(Move to the center.)*

That Jesus loved his friends. *(Move back out to the circle.)*

🦋 A Last Command 🦋

by Denise Harris

Love one another as I have loved you.
This was one of Jesus' last commands.
Yet do we really love one another?
And if so, why is it that
we make fun of the girl with crooked teeth
or the boy with the limp?
Why is it that
we say hurtful things about one another
or turn our backs on someone in need?
How can we live in his love and yet
be so unmoved by the suffering around us?
Jesus left no room for misunderstanding
in this final command.
And to demonstrate this love,
he washed his disciples' feet.
Love one another as I have loved you.
Can the meaning be any clearer?
Can the example set be any more pure?
Love one another as I have loved you.

❧ Breaking Bread ❧

by Nate Lee

Characters

Jesus	Peter
James	John
Owner	Disciples
Judas	Man with water

Props

any kind of clay jar or pot

lightweight table

chairs

one cup

round loaf of bread

Open with lots of people walking back and forth carrying jars of water, blankets, baskets, and other things. Peter and John enter.

John: What did Jesus say again?

Peter: He said to look for a guy carrying water.

John: Okayyyyy. I'm looking. Did he happen to say which guy?

Peter: Jesus said we'd know him when we saw him.

John: It's amazing how Jesus knows this stuff.

Peter: Amen, Brother.

Man with water jar comes up from behind and taps them on the shoulders, startling them.

Peter and John: Agggh!

Man with water: The Master sent you?

Peter: Yes.

Man with water: Follow me.

They follow the man, walking through the crowd of people carrying water and other things.

John: Where are we going?

Peter: Jesus said he would lead us to the house where we should have Passover supper.

They walk around and then come to the Owner who is standing in a doorway.

Man with water: This is the house.

John: Thank you, Sir.

Peter: *(to Owner)* Our Master sent us. He said you would have a room for us for our Passover supper.

Owner: The room is upstairs. It is ready for you.

As Peter and John climb fake stairs or climb onto risers, everyone else brings out the table and chairs and sets them up in the long fashion that we are used to seeing. It is okay if it takes awhile. Place the one cup and a loaf of bread at the end. Everyone is gathered in small groups, talking anxiously about Jesus.

Disciples: What do you think? / He's been acting very strangely, don't you think? / I don't get it. / He said he won't be with us soon. / He said he's going away? / What do you think he means?

Jesus enters, and all fall silent, except John and Peter.

John: Master! Welcome!

Peter: Jesus! I hope this room and meal please you.

Jesus: Thank you, Peter. Thank you, John. Yes, it is very nice. Please, everyone, sit down. I have something to tell you.

They all sit down.

John: What is it, Jesus?

Jesus: It is this: One of you will betray me this very night.

All disciples: *(scattered)* No! Not me! Is it me? Am I the one?

Jesus: I must die!

All: No!

Jesus: Yes! I must! I am the one the prophets wrote about hundreds of years ago. My Father sent me here for this purpose. But the man who betrays me . . . it will be much, much worse for him.

Judas: It is me, isn't it, Teacher?

Jesus: Yes, Judas. It is you. Go now and do what you must do.

Judas leaves.

James: I don't understand. How could you let him do that to you, Lord?

Jesus: It is God's will, James. I must fulfill the prophesy of the Messiah.

Jesus picks up the bread.

Jesus: *(in prayer)* Thank you, God, for this bread that we are about to eat.

Jesus breaks it apart, takes a piece, and passes out the rest.

Jesus: It is like this bread. My body is given up for you. For everyone. Take it and eat it.

Have each disciple taste the bread. Jesus takes the cup of wine.

Jesus: *(in prayer)* Thank you, God, for this wine we are about to drink.

Jesus takes a sip and then passes it on to the disciples.

Jesus: *(to the disciples)* Think of this wine as my blood. Soon, it will be poured out so that yours and everyone's sins will be forgiven. That is the sacrifice I must make.

All: No! No, Master! It can't be!

Jesus: It must be. But then, mark my words. We will drink wine again together some day in heaven.

Peter: Amen.

All: Amen.

Jesus and the disciples could sing a hymn or a song, or Jesus could leave and then they all leave.

 Could It Be?

by Michael Williams

Characters

Narrator	Chorus (Spoken)	Luke
James	Nathanael	Bartholomew
Matthew	Thomas	Judas
John	Philip	Peter
Mark	Andrew	Reader 1
Reader 2	Reader 3	Reader 4

Narrator: Reclining around a table on a holy, holy night, a rabbi and his disciples talked. The rabbi stopped the conversation with a startling revelation.

Chorus: "One of you will betray me," he said.

"One of you will deny me," he thought.

"All of you will desert me," echoed his broken heart.

Narrator: Those disciples who were able tried to rise above their fright. The rabbi watched as his disciples balked at the idea that one of them could hurt him—that they could betray, deny, desert him.

Chorus: "One of you will betray me," he said.

"One of you will deny me," he thought.

"All of you will desert me," echoed his broken heart.

Matthew: Could it be me?

John: Could it be me?

Mark: Could it be me?

Luke: Could it be me?

Nathanael: Could it be me?

Thomas: Could it be me?

Philip: Could it be me?

Andrew: Could it be me?

James: Could it be me?

Bartholomew: Could it be me?

Judas: Could it be me?

Peter: It could not be me. Which of the others?

Narrator: "Before the rooster crows, you will say you do not know me three times," Jesus said. "For days, every time the rooster crows, you'll be reminded of the words you could not say."

Reader 1: The woman approached and stared at Peter, "You're one of them." The woman spoke even louder this time. "You're one of them." The people around him leaned in to listen. "Is he one of them?" The people around him waited to hear. "Is he one of them?"

Chorus: No, I do not know him.

I do not know the man, I say.

Please, just get out of here.

Please, just go away.

Reader 2: The crowd began to grumble, "You're one of them." The very night seemed to question, "Is he one of them?" The silence around seemed to echo, "Is he one of them?"

Chorus: No, I do not know him.

I do not know the man, I say.

Please, just get out of here.

Please, just go away.

Reader 3: "You're one of them." The woman's voice repeated, "You're one of them." Peter found it hard to breathe. "Is he one of them?" His sweat cut icy rivers down his neck. "Is he one of them?"

Chorus: No, I do not know him.

I do not know the man, I say.

Please, just get out of here.

Please, just go away.

Reader 4: The rooster crowed as if to say, "You're one of them." A new voice came to question, "Are you one of them?" It was the voice of Jesus asking, "Are you one of them?"

Chorus: No, I do not know him.

I do not know this Jesus, I say.

Please, just let me get out of here.

Just let me go away.

❧ In the Garden ❧
by Linda Crooks

Characters

Reader 1	Reader 2	Reader 3
Reader 4	Reader 5	Reader 6

Reader 1: Jesus knew what was about to happen. He really didn't want to die.

Everyone: Not what I want, but what God wants.

Reader 2: So with his friends Peter, James, and John, Jesus went to the garden to pray.

Everyone: Not what I want, but what God wants.

Reader 3: Jesus knew that there was danger afoot tonight. He asked his friends to keep watch.

Everyone: Not what I want, but what God wants.

Reader 4: When Jesus was apart from his friends, he threw himself down on the ground.

Everyone: Not what I want, but what God wants.

Reader 5: "God, I am sad. I am frightened. You, who can do anything, can make this go away. But not what I want, but what you want."

Everyone: Not what I want, but what God wants.

Reader 6: Jesus got up and went to find his friends. They were sound asleep.

Everyone: Not what I want, but what God wants.

Reader 1: Jesus scolded them. "Can't you stay awake for even one hour? Your spirit is willing, but your body is weak."

Everyone: Not what I want, but what God wants.

Reader 2: Jesus returned to the garden and prayed. "I don't want to do this. But it's not what I want, but what you want."

Everyone: Not what I want, but what God wants.

Reader 3: And when Jesus returned to find his friends sleeping, he scolded, "We don't have time for taking a rest! The time is here!"

Everyone: Not what I want, but what God wants.

Reader 4: Judas led the soldiers into the garden. He went up to Jesus and kissed him.

Everyone: Not what I want, but what God wants.

Reader 5: The soldiers fell upon Jesus. One of Jesus' friends drew his sword and attacked one of the soldiers, cutting off his ear.

Everyone: Not what I want, but what God wants.

Reader 6: But Jesus asked them, "Why do you come here at night with swords and clubs as though I were a thief? Every day I have been in the Temple teaching."

Everyone: Not what I want, but what God wants.

Reader 1: And all of them ran away, leaving Jesus to the soldiers.

(Based on Mark 14:32-51.)

❧ Thank You ❧

by Alex Petrounov

Thank you, Jesus, for the truth you teach me!
Thank you, Jesus, for the good things you give me!
Thank you, Jesus, for going through the hard things
that you went through for me!
Thank you, Jesus, for not giving up!
Thank you, Jesus, for thinking about me!
Thank you, Jesus, for loving me so much!
Thank you, Jesus, for dying for me!
Thank you, God, for Jesus!

❧ Garden of Gethsemane ❧

by Nate Lee

Characters

Jesus	Slave	James
Peter	John	Guards
Disciples	Priests	Lieutenant
Judas	Crowd	

Props

If you have older children in this drama, create clubs and swords from cardboard and foil. If you have younger children in this drama, let them pretend to use clubs and swords.

Very dark stage. Peter and Jesus are walking together. James and John are a little behind. The mood is very quiet. Peter looks around, nervously.

Peter: A very dark night tonight. Very dark.

Jesus: Yes, it is.

Peter: Usually the garden of Gethsemane is beautiful…

Jesus: Yes.

Peter: But tonight, it seems . . . different.

Jesus: You are troubled by what I said at supper, Peter.

Peter: Jesus, I will stay by you—in prison—even to death!

Jesus: I am sorry to tell you this, Peter, but you will deny you even know me.

Peter: No! Not me, Master. Never!

Jesus: You will deny me three times, Peter. This very night, before the cock crows.

Peter: I will never deny you, Lord. Never.

Jesus: Wait here with the others, Peter. Keep watch. I must go pray.

(Peter sits with the other two. Jesus moves to the other side of the stage.)

Jesus: *(praying)* My Father, if it is your will, please let this cup—this duty—be taken from me. *(pauses silently, listening)* I want to do your will, not mine.

(Jesus pauses a moment, gathers his strength, then gets up. Jesus returns to the disciples, who are sleeping. He looks at them, sleeping, and shakes his head sadly.)

Jesus: *(quietly)* Peter? James? John?

(They awake with a start, even though Jesus spoke quietly.)

Peter: Master. Oh. Uhhh . . . I must have. . . .

Jesus: You couldn't even stay awake an hour with me? The spirit is willing, but the flesh is weak.

James: We're sorry, Lord.

John: It's been a very long day, Master. And it's so dark. . . .

Jesus: *(hears something)* Get up! The betrayer is here!

(The disciples rise. Judas enters, followed by priests and guards with swords and clubs. He comes up to Jesus.)

Judas: *(kissing Jesus on the cheek)* Teacher!

Jesus: You betray the Messiah with a kiss, Judas?

Lieutenant: Arrest that man!

(A few guards move forward.)

Peter: You will never take him!

(James, Peter, and John draw their swords. They fight with some of the mob. Suddenly, Peter takes a big swipe near a slave's ear.)

Slave: Aggggh! My ear! My ear! You've cut it off!

Jesus: Put your swords down! *(holds onto the slave's cut-off ear)* You live by the sword, you will die by the sword. *(Jesus heals the man's ear.)*

Slave: *(holding his hand over his ear)* It's all better! He fixed it! It's a miracle! *(Members of the crowd gasp in amazement.)*

Crowd: Did you see that? / He cured him. / I heard about such things. / It's a miracle! / It really is a miracle! / This Jesus of Nazareth / I can hardly believe it. / Better not tell anyone. / Maybe we should go!

Jesus: *(to the crowd)* You come here in the dead of night? What are you afraid of? You saw me at the Temple. You listened to me teach there. But you did not arrest me then.

(The guards back away. Others turn away, ashamed.)

Jesus: The priests among you. You study the Scripture. Know then that you are fulfilling it. Know that this was foretold by the prophets.

Priest: That is blasphemy!

Lieutenant: Arrest him. Now!

(The guards take Jesus, and the mob exits. The disciples are stunned. The slave holds back a bit.)

Slave: *(to the disciples and to himself)* Your master. He touched me. My ear. He spoke, and we couldn't even lift our swords. *(He lets the sword slowly drop out of his hand.)* He fixed... He fixed me. Just like that. It's true then. He is... He is....

(The slave runs after the mob.)

James: Look. He forgot his sword.

Peter: Me too. *(He throws his sword on the ground next to the slave's and exits in a different direction.)*

James and John look at each other. They throw their swords down, too, then exit in Peter's direction.

🦋 Jesus Before the Council 🦋

by James Ritchie

For Voice Choir

All: They took Jesus to the high priest;

Group 1: where all the chief priests,

Group 2: the elders,

Group 3: and the scribes

All: were assembled.

Voice 1: Peter had followed at a distance, right into the courtyard of the high priest; he was sitting with the guards, warming himself at the fire.

Group 1: Now the chief priests

Group 2: and the whole council

Group 3: were looking for testimony against Jesus

All: to put him to death,

Groups 1 & 2: but

Groups 2 & 3: they

Groups 1 & 3: found

Voice 2: none.

All: None?

Voice 2: None.

Group 1: For many gave false testimony against him, and their testimony did not agree.

Group 2: *(Start when Group 1 says, "against.")* For many gave false testimony against him, and their testimony did not agree.

Group 3: *(Start when Group 2 says, "against.")* For many gave false testimony against him, and their testimony did not agree.

All: We heard him say,

Group 3: "I will destroy this temple that is made with hands, and in three days, I will build another, not made with hands."

Group 1: But even on this point, their testimony did not agree.

Group 2: *(Start when Group 1 says, "their.")* But even on this point, their testimony did not agree.

Group 3: *(Start when Group 2 says, "their.")* But even on this point, their testimony did not agree.

Voice 1: Then the high priest stood up before them and asked Jesus,

All: "Have you no answer? What is it that they testify against you?"

Voice 2: But he was silent and did not answer.

Voice 1: Again the high priest asked him,

All: "Are you the Messiah, the Son of the Blessed One?"

Group 1: Jesus said,

Group 2: Jesus said,

Group 3: Jesus said,

Voice 3: "I am," and, "You will see the Son of Man seated at the right hand of the power."

All: Then the high priest tore his clothes

Group 1: *(Tear cloth.)*

Group 2: *(Tear cloth.)*

Group 3: *(Tear cloth.)*

All: and said,

Group 1: "Why do we still need witnesses?

Group 2: "You have heard this blasphemy!

Group 3: "What is your decision?"

All: All of them condemned him as deserving death,

Group 1: death,

Group 2: death,

Group 3: death.

Voice 1: Some began to spit on him,

Voice 2: to blindfold him,

Voice 3: and to strike him, saying to him,

Voice 1: "Prophesy!

Group 1: "Prophesy!

Voice 2: "Prophesy!

Group 2: "Prophesy!

Voice 3: "Prophesy!

Group 3: "Prophesy!

All: "Prophesy!" The guards also took him over and beat him.

Voice 3: *(Hit fists into hands loudly.)*

Group 1: *(Hit fists into hands loudly.))*

Group 2: *(Hit fists into hands loudly.)*

Group 3: *(Hit fists into hands loudly.)*

All: *(Hit fists into hands loudly.)*

✂ That They May ALL Be One ✂

by Linda Whited

Production Notes

This is a monologue with an introduction and some additional remarks made by a narrator. The narrator does not need to appear on stage. Jesus may be spotlighted, kneeling in prayer. For older teens and adults.

Characters

Narrator	Jesus

Narrator: As he thought about the hours ahead, Jesus prayed. First, he prayed for himself:

Jesus: Father, the time has come for all that you have planned to be accomplished. You sent me into the world to bring the good news to every person; to tell them that they could know eternal life by knowing you and by knowing me, the one you sent to teach them. I have given glory to you by doing all that you told me to do. I am ready now for the glory we shared before the world was created to be revealed.

Narrator: Jesus thought about his disciples. They had been his closest friends and traveling companions. He loved each one of them and wanted only the best for them. He knew that they would have to be strong and that they would need God's help. Jesus prayed for the disciples:

Jesus: I have told my disciples all about you. They know that all I have said to them comes as a gift from you. They have accepted your commandments and believe that you sent me.

I pray for the disciples you have given to me. I am leaving the world soon to come to you, but I will leave my disciples here in the world. While I have been with them, I have kept them safe. Now keep them in your care. Help them to be united in their love for me and for you.

I told my disciples many things while I was with them so that they could be filled with joy. They have heard and accepted your commands. Now sometimes it is hard for them to fit in with the world. I am not asking you to take them out of this world, but I am asking you to protect them as they face the troubles that will surely come. Set them apart for your sacred use. I send them out into the world just like you sent me into the world. And for them, I dedicate myself to you so that they may be truly dedicated to you.

Narrator: It was such a long time ago, and yet Jesus prayed for us too:

Jesus: My prayer is not just for these who have been my disciples, but for all the believers who will follow me because of those disciples.

The world does not know you, but I know you and all of my disciples know that you sent me. I will continue to love them so that the love you have given me will also be in them, and I will be in them too.

Narrator: *(Pray)* Gracious God, thank you for sending Jesus into the world to save us from our sins. Help us to live the way he taught his disciples to live. Amen.

🦋 Kindness Is What God Wants 🦋
by LeeDell Stickler

"How much more worth is a person
Than a goat or a cow or a sheep?
It is right to do good on the sabbath.
That's the one rule it's all right to keep."
But the Pharisees muttered and mumbled.
They were angry at what Jesus said.
They whispered together and plotted,
For these men would see Jesus dead.
We know that God's love is for always;
Do good every day of the week.
God wants us to live just like Jesus,
Showing kindness to all that we meet.
The Scriptures say treat all with kindness.
Don't be afraid to open your heart.
Share all the kindness inside you,
And that's a pretty good start.

❧ Mystery of the Shaking Ground ❧

by LeeDell Stickler

Characters

Child	Baker	Mother
Woman at the Well	Mary Magdalene	Potter
Cloth Dyer	Mary	Merchant

Props

Mother: straw carry basket for market day

Potter: straw mat, clay pots

Cloth Dyer: vat of liquid, cloth

Merchant: produce, straw mat

Baker: basket of bread

Woman at the Well: clay water jar

Setting

It is early in the morning, just at daybreak in the city of Jerusalem. It is the day after the sabbath and the Passover. During the Passover, Jesus had been crucified and buried in Joseph of Arimathea's tomb. The city is nervous and anxious to get back to normal. A mother and her child have come early to the market to purchase food after the sabbath.

Sound

Sound of the earthquake. (Group of children sitting in chairs stomping feet, making the stage shake.)

Child: *(grabs mother's tunic and tries to hide behind her)* Mother, what was that? It felt as though the earth was rolling and rumbling under my feet. I felt as though I was going to fall down. I wonder if other people felt it too.

Mother: I've never felt that before. Why don't you ask some of the people here in the marketplace? It's a mystery to me.

Child: *(walks to where the Potter is setting pots on a straw mat)* Potter, my mother and I have just come to the marketplace. But as we walked, we felt the earth rolling and rumbling beneath our feet. This has never happened before. Do you know what has happened? It's a mystery to me!

Potter: I was setting out my pots in the marketplace. I wanted an early start. It's the day after the sabbath and bound to be a busy one in the marketplace. There was such a crowd in the city for the Passover. Before they head back to their villages, I'm bound to sell a lot of pots. Just as I was setting them out, two of my pots fell off the shelf and broke. I looked to see if someone had been careless. But that wasn't it. It felt as though the very earth beneath my feet was shivering and shaking. I can't help you. It's a mystery to me.

Child: *(walks up to the Cloth Dyer who is dipping a red cloth in a vat of red dye and wringing it out)* Cloth Dyer, my mother and I have just come to the marketplace. But as we walked, we felt the earth rolling and rumbling beneath our feet. The Potter says he felt the earth shivering and shaking. This has never happened before. Do you know what has happened? It's a mystery to me!

Cloth Dyer: *(pulls cloth from vat of dye and wrings it out and hangs it up to dry)* I was mixing my vat of dye for my cloth. I've heard that the curtain in the Temple was ripped from top to bottom on Friday. I want to be prepared if the high priest wants another one. That's when the dye in my vat sloshed over onto the ground. Now I'm not sure there will be enough. It felt like the earth was quivering and quaking.

Child: *(to the Merchant who is setting out his fruits and vegetables)* Merchant, my mother and I have just come to the marketplace. But as we walked, we felt the earth rolling and rumbling beneath our feet. The Potter says he felt the earth shivering and shaking. The Cloth Dyer said he felt the earth quivering and quaking. This has never happened before. Do you know what has happened? It's a mystery to me!

Merchant: At first I thought it was a Roman legion marching through the marketplace. There have been many soldiers in Jerusalem for the Passover. I think they were expecting trouble from Jesus and his disciples. I was almost afraid to set out my apples and pomegranates. I just knew the horses would stampede through the market and trample all my beautiful produce. But I waited and nothing more happened. But it felt as though the earth was rocking and rattling.

Child: *(to the Baker who is setting out baskets of bread)* Baker, my mother and I have just come to the marketplace. But as we walked, we felt the earth rolling and rumbling beneath our feet. The Potter says he felt the earth shivering and shaking. The Cloth Dyer said he felt the earth quivering and quaking. The Merchant said he felt the earth rocking and rattling. This has never happened before. Do you know what has happened? It's a mystery to me!

Baker: I heard it too. I had stirred up the fire in my oven way before the sun came up. Now that the sabbath is over, there will be many people who will want my loaves of bread. The first batch was just about ready and I was removing the loaves from the heated stones when I felt it. I almost dropped the loaves onto the coals in the bottom of the oven. It felt like the earth was tossing and turning.

Child: *(to the Woman at the Well)* Woman, my mother and I have just come to the marketplace. But as we walked, we felt the earth rolling and rumbling beneath our feet. The Potter says he felt the earth shivering and shaking. The Cloth Dyer said he felt the earth quivering and quaking. The Baker said he felt the earth tossing and turning. The Merchant says he felt the earth rocking and rattling. This has never happened before. Do you know what has happened? It's a mystery to me!

Woman at the Well: *(setting her jar on the ground)* I heard it and felt it. Just as I was coming back from the well with a full jar of water, the earth began to shudder and sway. I thought I would fall to the ground if I hadn't found a tree branch to hold on to. At least I wasn't the only one who felt it. There were several of us who had come to the well to get water this early in the morning before the sun becomes too hot.

Child: *(to Mary Magdalene and the other Mary)* Mary Magdalene and Mary, my mother and I have just come to the marketplace. But as we walked, we felt the earth rolling and rumbling beneath our feet. The Potter says he felt the earth shivering and shaking. The Cloth Dyer said he felt the earth quivering and quaking. The Baker said he felt the earth tossing and trembling. The Merchant says he felt the earth rocking and rattling. The Woman at the Well said she felt the earth shudder and sway. This has never happened before. Do you know what has happened? It's a mystery to me!

Mary Magdalene: It's not a mystery to me. I know what happened! Mary and I were on our way to the tomb where they had laid our friend and teacher, Jesus. On Thursday night, he had been arrested and tried by the council. Then the Roman governor, Pilate, sentenced him to die on a cross. Joseph had a tomb in a garden that he let them use to bury Jesus. Mary and I were on our way to prepare his body for a proper burial. That's when it happened.

Child: That's when the earth rolled and rumbled? That's when the earth shivered and shook? That's when the earth quivered and quaked? That's when the earth tossed and trembled? That's when the earth rocked and rattled? That's when the earth shuddered and swayed?

Mary: Yes, but it wasn't an earthquake at all. It was an angel. When the angel came down from heaven, it made the sound as it rolled back the stone that sealed the tomb.

Mary Magdalene: A good thing, too, because the stone was very heavy. We could never have moved that stone by ourselves.

Mary: The angel told us not to be afraid. He knew that we were looking for Jesus. But the angel knew that Jesus wasn't there. That's why he was sitting there—to tell us the wonderful news.

Mary Magdalene: God has raised Jesus from the dead. The angel even invited us to look inside to see for ourselves.

Mary: When we saw the linen cloths lying where Jesus had been only two days before, we knew. Jesus is alive!

Child: There is no mystery?

Mary Magdalene: There is no mystery. Just news of great joy. Jesus is alive!

Everyone: Jesus is alive!

✤ Pass It On ✤

by Shelba Shelton Nivens

Production Notes

This is a dramatization of the women at the empty tomb, to begin a service of joy and celebration on Easter Sunday. It is designed for easy production. Few props are needed.

Characters

Mary Magdalene	Other Mary
Salome	Angel

Costumes

White robe for Angel. Biblical dress for women.

Props and Scenery

Baskets and jars for the women. Tomb is painted on a free-standing screen. Potted plants can represent the garden.

Tomb is downstage left. Mary Magdalene, Other Mary, and Salome enter from stage right with baskets and jars of spices and ointments.

Salome: How can the day dawn so beautiful and bright as this when there is so much darkness within our souls?

Mary Magdalene: I feel as though my world ended with Jesus.

Other Mary: He brought such hope into our lives. Everyone said he was to be our Savior or Deliverer. Why, I, myself, had hopes of my own two sons, James and John, sitting one on his left and the other on his right when he came into his kingdom. But now he is dead. All hope is gone.

Mary Magdalene: I feel that I just cannot bear it. It was he who gave me my life again. Demons had destroyed me. I was tortured day and night. I wanted only to die. And then I heard about this man called Jesus.... *(breaks down crying)*

Salome: *(places arm around Mary Magdalene)* We all are sorely grieved over what has happened. He was my own dear sister Mary's son, you know. How it hurts me to look upon her sadness. She was standing right there near the cross, witnessing his agony, when he died. *(cries into her shawl)*

Other Mary: But we must not stand here weeping. This is the dawn of the third day. The law of the sabbath has already prevented a proper burial. We must prepare his body right away. *(looks in basket)* Mary, did you bring the special ointment we prepared?

Mary Magdalene: *(drying eyes)* I have it. But here—you take it, Mary. *(gives bottle to Mary)* I don't think I can bear to look upon his poor, lifeless form again.

Other Mary: *(briskly)* Of course you can. Did we not all minister to him in life? This one last thing we shall all do together for him also.

Mary Magdalene: You are right. I must do this for him. But hurry, so we may finish this sad work as quickly as possible. *(looks around)* I was certain it was near this spot that they laid him.

Salome: He was laid in the new tomb over there. *(indicates direction)* My eyes were dimmed by tears, but I made special note of the spot so I could return with spices.

(Mary Magdalene moves sadly to the tomb.)

Other Mary: But, Salome, a heavy stone was rolled over the opening. I heard that the soldiers sealed it in place. How shall we roll it away?

Salome: Perhaps we should have asked one of the men to...

Mary Magdalene: *(from the tomb)* Mary! Salome! Come quickly! The stone has been rolled away.

Other Mary, Salome: *(look at each other in surprise.)* But...who could have done it? What does it mean?

Mary Magdalene: *(bends to look inside the tomb)* Oh, no-o-o-o! He is not here! He is gone!

Salome: Gone? He can't be! *(hurries to look inside the tomb)*

Other Mary: *(hurries to look inside the tomb)* It is true. He is gone!

(Women stare at each other in surprise, start to cry.)

Angel: *(enters from behind the tomb)* Why are you crying?

Mary Magdalene: *(wails)* Because they have taken away the body of my Lord—and I don't know where they have laid him.

Other Mary: It is an angel of the Lord!

(Women fall to their knees.)

Angel: Do not be afraid. Get up. Are you looking for Jesus, the Nazarene who was crucified?

(Women rise.)

Mary Magdalene: Yes, but we cannot find him.

Angel: Why are you so surprised? Did he not tell you that the Messiah would be betrayed into the power of evil men and be crucified? And that he would rise again after three days?

Other Mary: *(nodding slowly)* Yes, he did tell us that.

Salome: It was back in Galilee...

Mary Magdalene: I remember...

Angel: Then why are you here looking in a tomb for someone who is alive? Jesus is not here. He has come back to life.

Salome: *(in awe)* My sister's son is alive? He is actually the Messiah?

Other Mary: *(in awe)* Jesus? The Messiah? The Deliverer?

Mary Magdalene: *(joyfully)* Yes! Oh, yes! It is true! I know it is true. Jesus is the Messiah! The Savior! My Lord! And he is alive!

Other Mary, Salome: Jesus has risen! He lives!

Angel: Then go and tell his disciples. He will meet you in Galilee, just as he told you before he died.

Other Mary: Yes! We must tell the others. I must tell my sons.

Salome: I must tell his mother, my sister.

Mary Magdalene: We must tell everyone. Jesus lives!

(Women hurry joyfully down the aisle, exclaiming loudly to the people in the congregation right and left.)

Jesus is alive!

He lives!

Pass it on!

Tell your neighbor!

Tell everyone!

He's the Messiah!

He's the Savior!

He is Lord!

He lives!

He lives forever!

Choir: *(Joyful music such as "He Lives.")*

 This Song

by Nate Lee

I've seen a thousand lilies
Gathering to play
A triumphant trumpet chorus
Heralding the day!
The song's the purest, clearest
And bright as whitest light
Spreading 'round the world
It overwhelms the night!
Our joy arises, resounding
As all who hear sing out
Allelu-Leuia!
Let the Truth ring out!
Allelu-Leuia!
All things made anew
Allelu-Leuia!
This song given to you!

🦋 The Underground Resurrection 🦋

by Valeria Steele Roberson

Characters

Harriet Tubman: A former slave who went South numerous times to deliver others from slavery
Louisa: A young slave girl who is very curious
Clara: Louisa's very emotional mother
Charles: A young slave who was whipped many times by his master
MacRay: An older slave who is very wise
Ruth: A character from the Bible (can be played by a teen)
Isaiah: An ex-slave named after the character from the Bible
Daniel: A character from the Bible
Nonspeaking Parts: Mary Magdalene; Salome; Mary, mother of James; Angel

Props

Harriet's knapsack that includes a loaf of bead, a water container, a jar of salve, and a gun

Bale of hay

Shoes for Charles

Blankets

Old rags for bandages

Basket full of food and water containers

Scene 1

(The play opens as Harriet and her passengers are trying to hide from slave catchers. They're hiding in a barn with a concealed floor at the William Randolph farm in Buffalo, New York. Place a bale of hay at right. It is sunrise on Friday, two days before Easter, and everybody is asleep. Harriet wakes up and moves stage right away from the group and begins praying into a hole in the ground.)

Harriet: Oh, Lord, I need you to help us. Lord, we thank you for allowing us to reach this safe place in Buffalo, New Yawk. You done brought us all the way from Maryland. And, Lord, now we's so close. Just a few more miles 'til we gets to Canada, to freedom. Please guide us to safety, Lord. Let your North Star shine! We thank you for deliverance right now. In the sweet name of Jesus, your Son and our miracle worker, I pray. Amen. *(MacRay wakes and walks over to her.)*

MacRay: Can't sleep. Miss Harriet?

Harriet: Too excited. First of all, I'm happy that y'all gonna be free. An' second, this marks two days before Easter Sunday morning. I don't like thinking too much 'bout Jesus sufferin' on the cross. But what comes after makes me want to shout.

MacRay: Jesus done rose from the grave. Miss Harriet, knowing Jesus was the onliest thing kept me going all of these years. *(Louisa wakes up and then wakes up her mother.)*

Louisa: Mama, I had a bad dream. They caught us and... *(She begins to cry.)*

Clara: Don't cry, baby girl. We's safe here in Mr. Randolph's barn. Don't nobody know 'bout this room hidden 'neath his barn. And don't you know that Miss Harriet ain't never got caught? An' she never will. *(Charles thrashes and talks in his sleep.)*

Charles: Yessir, master, I ain't gonna do it no mo'. *(Clara shakes him out of his sleep.)*

Clara: Wake up, Charles, it's all right. You won't have to be scared no mo' when we get to Canada.

Charles: I sho' hope so. *(Harriet and MacRay walk over to them. Harriet offers them all a piece of bread to munch on and some water.)*

Louisa: Thanks, Miss Harriet. *(Others say thanks too.)*

Harriet: Y'all go on back to sleep. Tonight we be travelin' in the back of a wagon most of the night.

Louisa: Miss Harriet, will you tell us a story?

(As Harriet enacts the story at left, actors can be acting it out at right.)

Harriet: A story. Well, since it's Easter time, I'll tell you 'bout the women who ran to the tomb early that blessed Sunday mornin'. There was Mary Magdalene, Salome, and the other Mary who went there to anoint the body of Jesus. But what they found instead was God's miracle. You see, there was a great earthquake, and an angel rolled the stone away an' told 'em not to be afraid. Say, "Jesus is not here, for he done rose up!" After they saw that he wasn't there, the angel told 'em to tell the rest of 'em, you know, the men folk, the good news. And they ran to tell 'em.

MacRay: Sho' 'nuff. Only a powerful God like ourns could have done sumpin' like that.

Harriet: But that's not all. The Bible says that some of God's saints who had been asleep got up after Jesus rose and walked around the city an' appeared to people.

Charles: Are you saying that dead folk got up and walked around? *(Harriet nods yes.)* That must have been a sight.

Harriet: Now, Charles, they wasn't trying to scare nobody. They were just witnessin' to God's power. *(Charles yawns.)*

Charles: I better get me some more shut-eye.

Louisa: I'm sleepy too. *(Louisa and Charles go back to their pallets.)*

Harriet: I guess that Charles don't believe that God can work a miracle.

MacRay: Well, I know God can.

Clara: I believe God can do anything. This is God's world.

Harriet: I had one of my sleeping fits a few weeks back; and whilst I was in it, I had a dream. I was in a dark place. All'a sudden, a light shone brightly in the distance. I walked toward that light, and there she stood.

Clara: Who?

Harriet: Ruth! She's one of my favorite Bible people because our stories are sort of alike. It takes a lot of faith to leave the known for the unknown. Anyway, this is what I heard and saw. *(Ruth enters from left. Harriet rises and joins her. She sits down before Ruth.)*

Ruth: Keep looking up to God, Harriet. God'll be there for you, just like God was there for my dear, sweet mother-in-law, Naomi, and me.

Harriet: God helped you do the right thing for your life, didn't God?

Ruth: God sure did. I loved my mother-in-law, Naomi, so much. When she told me she was returning to Bethlehem, I knew I had to go with her. By that time, I realized who God was. I knew I could depend on God. So I took a step in faith, and God blessed me beyond my imagination. You just never know what will happen when you serve the true and living God.

Harriet: Is it true that you were resurrected with Jesus?

Ruth: Oh, yes, Harriet. I was there on that happy day. We walked around Jerusalem telling everybody we saw about God's awesome power. Be encouraged, dear sister. Keep trusting in God. *(She exits right and then Harriet rejoins the others and sits down.)*

Harriet: Then I woke up.

Clara: Our God is still in the miracle-making business. Please, Lord, help us just like you helped Ruth.

MacRay: Praise be to God.

Harriet: We'd better get some sleep. We got a long night ahead. *(Blackout or play music to indicate the change of scenes.)*

SCENE 2

(It's Saturday, the next evening. It's the night before Easter. Harriet and the others are moving up Freedom's Highway through the bushes.)

Clara: I don't means to complain or nothin', but it sho' was nice to travel in that wagon last night.

Louisa: I'm so tired, Mama.

Harriet: I know y'all is tired. We don't have that much farther to go. Our next stop is on top of that hill.

Clara: Thank goodness. Don't know if'n I can walk much farther. My feets hurtin' already!

Charles: Me neither. I can see it. *(Points right.)* Come on, y'all, I'm hungry.

Harriet: Get back in line.

Charles: Why? We can see it ain't far. *(Harriet pulls out her gun.)*

Harriet: I'm not lettin' you mess this up. Get back. Shh!

MacRay: What is it, Harriet?

Harriet: Just a feeling. Let's hide over there. *(They move left and pretend like they're hiding. Then they hear horses on the road. Harriet moves right and looks where the horses are going.)* Oh, my Lord, that was too close for comfort. We'll wait here 'til it's good an' dark. Then I'll go and scout out the place. Have a seat, ev'rybody, and get comf'table.

Charles: I'm real sorry, Miss Harriet.

MacRay: He told you, didn't he?

Harriet: Yes, it was Jesus. I always get this feeling when danger is near.

Louisa: What does it feel like?

Harriet: I can't really explain it.

Clara: God will do that for God's chil'ren.

MacRay: Praise be to God. Takin' care of us, even when we act like we ain't got no sense.

Charles: I done said I was sorry. *(He steps on a spiny sweet gum ball.)* Oh, I...my foot.

Harriet: Shh. Shh. A burr got you. Let me take a look at your foot. It's pretty bad. I betta put some of my salve on that. *(She removes jar from bag and places some salve on his foot.)* You rest now. *(Charles lies down.)*

Charles: Those things sho' put a hurtin' on your foots. I gots to get me some shoes. Can't go no farther 'til I do.

Harriet: I'll see 'bout it in the mornin'. Too many slave catchers round now.

MacRay: It's always somethin' in dis here life. That's why the good Lawd says to take it one day at a time. Charles, we gwine get you just what you needs. God will see to it.

Harriet: Let's get comf'table.

Louisa: Miss Harriet, can you tell us a story?

Harriet: If you all don't mind hearing about some more Bible peoples, I can.

MacRay: Help yo'self.

Harriet: It seems like whenever I need some encouragement, God sends me somebody. One time God sent me one of the greatest prophets ever—Isaiah.

Louisa: Was he one of those saints who rose when Jesus rose from the dead?

Harriet: Sho' was. He believed mens should depend on God and not live by fear.

MacRay: Only a powerful God can raise people from the dead.

Clara: So what do you think Isaiah said to the people after he rose up?

Harriet: For one thing, Clara, I think he talked about how Jesus can heal these old bodies.

Clara: I wish.

MacRay: Don't it say in Isaiah: "By his stripes we are healed"? They sho' put a lot of them on him, too, before they nailed him to de cross. Jesus was beat just like we was. *(A man begins singing the spiritual, "Swing Low," off-stage right.)*

Harriet: Shh. Shh. Be very quiet. *(The man continues to sing. Harriet walks toward the singing. She exits right.)*

Clara: Lord, have mercy, where she done gone?

MacRay: It will be all right, Li'l Sister. *(Harriet enters, followed by Isaiah.)*

Harriet: Y'all, this here is Isaiah. Mr. Jones from up the road sent him down here to look for us. Ain't he a sight for sore eyes?

Isaiah: I got a wagon just a ways off through that brush over there. Follow me, and I take you to Mr. Jones's barn up on the hill.

Clara: God sho' answers prayers.

MacRay: Always on time. Here, lean on me, Charles.

Charles: Thank goodness. *(They follow Isaiah and exit right.)*

SCENE 3

(Harriet and the others follow Isaiah into Mr. Jones's barn. There are a few blankets scattered about. They sit around talking. Isaiah begins to laugh)

Isaiah: Y'all be safe here in Mr. Jones's barn. Right here is a basket full of food and water.

Harriet: Thank you so much, Isaiah. Ya'll, Isaiah been free 'bout ten years now.

Louisa: We almost free, too, ain't we, Mama?

Clara: Yea, that's right.

Isaiah: Ain't nothing like it. I still can't believe that you were just about to tell them about the prophet Isaiah when I showed up.

Louisa: How you get your name, Isaiah?

Isaiah: My mama named me after the prophet Isaiah. She loved all he had to say about Jesus. How Jesus loved the poor and cared about the brokenhearted. How he'd give sight to the blind and deliverance to captives. How he came to make a difference in people's lives. People like you and like me. You see, we know how all of that feels. We know about going without. But Jesus, he came to make life better for us all.

Clara: You sho' seem to know the Bible. Can you read?

Isaiah: Yes, ma'am, I sho' can.

Louisa: Mama, can I learn to read?

Isaiah: Child, you sho will. Just keep your hands in God's hands. All things are possible for God.

MacRay: Sho' nuff. 'Cause Jesus died on that cross.

Isaiah: He was despised and rejected by men, a bearer of our griefs and a carrier of our sorrows. He took it all on that cross with him. Yes, Jesus was our sin-bearing servant. Now that comes from the prophet Isaiah.

MacRay: And then Jesus rose again on the third day.

Isaiah: Yes, so it is by stripes we are healed.

   43

Harriet: See, Charles, Jesus will heal your feet. He can heal all of our illnesses. One time I was so sick, didn't nobody think I'd make it. So when all around you seems so dark in your life, have faith 'cause God can do ev'rything but fail.

MacRay: Amen.

Isaiah: *(He rises.)* Well, I better be goin'. Y'all are safe here. Just a few more miles, and y'all be in Canada. Y'all can leave here tomorrow night. Miss Harriet, y'all be careful now. God go with you.

Louisa: Thank you, Mr. Isaiah.

Isaiah: Y'all is welcome. God bless all of you. *(He exits right.)*

Harriet: Let's get some rest. *(They all go to sleep.)*

SCENE 4

(It's the next morning, Sunday, around dawn. All are still sleeping. Harriet enters from right with a pair of shoes and some food to eat.)

Harriet: It's another Easter mornin' sunrise and I'm glad 'bout it. Lawd, we just want to give you thanks for Jesus Christ who suffered, died, and rose from the grave. And Lawd, we thank you that this is Resurrection Day for all these chil'ren you give me to take across to the free side. In Jesus the Christ's name, we pray. Amen. *(The others start rising as Harriet moves closer to them.)*

MacRay: Miss Harriet, happy Easter Day.

Harriet: Same to you.

Louisa: Miss Harriet, tonight is the night, right?

Harriet: We almost there. I got y'all some food, and here's some water too. So eat up. Charles, here you some shoes.

Charles: Thank you, Miss Harriet.

Harriet: How your feet doin' today?

Charles: Why, Miss Harriet, they's just like new.

Harriet: I told you that Jesus is a healer.

MacRay: Amen. Always give us just what we need.

Clara: Are you sure we should try tonight?

Harriet: Child, we'll see. God didn't bring us this far to leave us.

MacRay: No, siree. No more slave days and slave ways. We be delivered, just like Daniel from the lions' den.

Louisa: Tell 'em, Miss Harriet, tell 'em.

Harriet: Louisa wants me to tell you about my dream about the prophet Daniel.

Louisa: And he rose on that day when Jesus rose, didn't he, Miss Harriet?

Harriet: Why, 'course he did. Daniel tried to encourage his people during a time when they were slaves, just like so many of our people are. One of his messages was that God...

MacRay: ...was still in control no mater what their lot in life.

Harriet: That's right.

Clara: That's good to hear.

Harriet: Better to know. We have to live by faith, not sight.

Charles: Tell us more about Daniel.

Harriet: When Daniel came upon some people after he'd risen from the dead, he had a very important message for them. *(Daniel enters from left.)*

Daniel: God is a good God. God delivered me again and again. Just look at me. I'm a living, breathing testimony of God's goodness once more in the land of the living. So don't be scared of me. I just got a few more things I'd like to tell you. Many years ago, I lived in exile in Babylon, and it was a very trying time for me and my friends. However, there is one time in particular that I'll never forget. One time I slept in the lions' den all night long. I ended up there because I prayed to my God three times a day. I didn't care about a new law that said I couldn't pray. And God shut the lions' jaws, and they left me alone. So I know that when you are faithful to God, He'll see you through. *(Daniel exits left.)*

MacRay: Amen.

Harriet: Isn't God good? It's just a few more hours' journey before y'all be in Canada. We'll leave when night falls. All I ask is that you all keep God first and always help somebody else in this life.

Louisa: We will, won't we, Mama? Miss Harriet, thank you so much for ev'rything. *(They all thank Miss Harriet.)*

Harriet: It's like the good book says, "A child shall lead them." God bless you, child. God bless you all. This Easter, y'all gonna be delivered! *(Starts singing, "They Rolled the Stone Away," or another song about Easter.)*

ꙮ Easter ꙮ
by Karen Williams

This is a group recitation with six children. Each child holds one letter of the word EASTER.

E: E is for Eternal life Jesus offers to those who will believe.

A: A is for All the miracles Jesus performed for those who would receive.

S: S is for the Soldiers who blocked his grave with a heavy stone.

T: T is for the Tomb where they placed Jesus. They thought he was dead and gone.

E: E is for Everyone—for all of us the cross Jesus bore.

R: R is for Resurrection—Jesus is alive forevermore!

✿ I Have Seen the Lord! ✿

by James Ritchie

Production Notes

You will need to make a representation of the empty tomb. Have the three groups stand where they will not be in the way of the actors entering and leaving the stage. Costumes can be as simple or as elaborate as you wish.

Characters

Groups 1, 2, and 3 to serve as a chorus		
Jesus	Mary Magdalene	Angel 1
Nonspeaking parts: Peter, John, Angel 2		

Group 1: Early!

Group 2: On the first day of the week.

Group 3: Early!

Group 1: While it was still dark.

Group 2: That early?

Group 3: That early!

Group 1: Mary Magdalene came to the tomb.

Group 2: Early!

Group 3: The stone had been rolled away!

Groups 1 & 2: *(Gasp!)*

Group 3: So she ran . . .

Group 2: . . . to find Peter and John . . .

Group 3: . . . and said to them,

Mary Magdalene: They have taken the Lord out of the tomb, and I do not know where they have laid him.

Group 1: Then Peter . . .

Group 2: . . . and John . . .

Groups 1 & 2: . . . set out and went toward the tomb.

Group 3: The two were running together.

Group 1: But John outran Peter and was the first one to the tomb.

Group 2: John bent down to look inside. He saw the linen wrappings lying there, but didn't go in.

Group 3: Then Peter came along and went immediately into the tomb.

Group 1: The linen wrappings were there.

Groups 1 & 2: But no Jesus!

Group 3: No Jesus?

Group 1: The cloth that covered Jesus' face was there, although it was rolled up and set aside.

Groups 1 & 2: But no Jesus!

Group 1: Then John went in.

Groups 2 & 3: He saw . . .

All: . . . and believed.

Group 1: Even though he didn't understand what he saw.

Group 2: Or the Scripture that said Jesus would rise from the dead.

All: Then the disciples returned to their homes.

Group 1: But Mary stood weeping outside the tomb.

Mary Magdalene: *(Weeping)*

Group 2: As she wept, she bent over to look in the tomb.

Group 3: She saw two angels in white, . . .

All: *(Gasp!)*

Group 3: . . . sitting where the body of Jesus had been lying, . . .

Group 1: . . . one at the head . . .

Group 2: . . . and one at the feet.

Groups 1 & 2: But no Jesus!

Mary Magdalene: *(Weeping)*

Angel 1: Woman, why are you weeping?

Mary Magdalene: They've taken away my Lord, and I don't know where they have laid him.

Group 3: After saying this,

Group 1: Mary turned around and saw Jesus standing there, . . .

All: Whoa!

Group 1: . . . but didn't realize who he was.

Jesus: Woman, why are you weeping? Whom are you looking for?

Group 1: Mary thought it was the gardener.

Group 2: The gardener?

Group 1: The gardener.

Group 3: Why the gardener?

Group 1: Well, she certainly wasn't expecting Jesus.

Mary Magdalene: Sir, if you have carried him away, tell me where you have laid him, and I will take him away.

Jesus: Mary!

Mary Magdalene: Teacher!

Jesus: Don't hold on to me, because I have not yet gone to be with the Father. But go, tell my brothers that I am going to be with my Father and your Father, to my God and your God.

Group 1: So Mary went . . .

Group 2: . . . and told the disciples what she had seen, . . .

Group 3: . . . saying to them, . . .

Mary Magdalene: . . . I have seen the Lord!

All: She has seen the Lord!

Group 1: That evening, on the first day of the week, . . .

Group 2: . . . when the disciples gathered behind locked doors, . . .

Group 3: . . . afraid of their own people, . . .

Group 1: . . . Jesus came and stood among them.

Jesus: Peace be with you.

Group 2: He showed them his hands and his side.

Group 3: The disciples rejoiced when they saw the Lord.

Mary Magdalene: We have seen the Lord!

All: We have seen the Lord!

❧ Going to the Tomb ❧
by Linda Ray Miller

Sing to the tune of "This Is the Way"

This is the way the women walked, *(walk in place)*
women walked, women walked.
This is the way the women walked, going to the tomb.

This is the way the women looked, *(look surprised)*
women looked, women looked.
This is the way the women looked inside the tomb.

This is the way the women ran, *(run in place)*
women ran, women ran.
This is the way the women ran to tell the good news.

Seven Miles From Jerusalem

by LeeDell Stickler

Characters

Narrator	Simon
Cleopas	Jesus

Props

small table and chairs

round, unbroken loaf of bread

(Scene opens with Simon and Cleopas walking side by side, talking quietly.)

Narrator: On the day that the women found the empty tomb, two other followers of Jesus were on their way to a village called Emmaus.

Simon: What do you think about the news?

Cleopas: You mean what the women reported when they went to the tomb?

Simon: That's exactly what I'm talking about. Could it be true?

Cleopas: I've never heard of anyone dying and coming back to life before.

Simon: But didn't Jesus tell us that this was going to happen?

(Jesus quietly enters stage and walks along beside the two men.)

Jesus: You men seem so intent on your conversation as you walk down the road. What are you talking about?

Cleopas: Are you the only stranger in Jerusalem who does not know the things that have taken place in these past few days?

Jesus: What things?

Simon: The things about Jesus of Nazareth, who was a prophet mighty in deed and word before God and all the people.

Cleopas: You have heard how our chief priests handed him over to Pilate to be put to death.

Simon: We had so hoped that he was the one to save our people.

Cleopas: But now it's the third day since these things took place. Some of our women are telling a wild tale about what they saw at his tomb this morning.

Simon: They said that his body was missing, and there were angels present who said that Jesus was alive.

Cleopas: Some went to the tomb to check it out. The tomb was empty and the burial cloths were lying there. But they didn't see Jesus.

Jesus: How foolish you are and how slow of heart to believe!

Narrator: Jesus began with Moses and all the prophets and explained to the men all the things about himself in all the Scriptures. Soon, they drew close to Emmaus.

Cleopas: Stay with us. It is almost evening and the day is nearly over.

Simon: It is not safe for a traveler on the road at night. We would like your company.

(Jesus, Simon, and Cleopas sit at the table. Jesus lifts the bread and breaks it.)

Narrator: They gathered at the table for the evening meal. Jesus took the bread, blessed it, broke it, and gave it to them. Then the men instantly recognized that it was Jesus.

(Jesus gets up quickly and exits.)

Cleopas: Where did he go? He was right here.

Simon: We should have known, as our hearts burned inside us at his words.

Cleopas: Let's go back to Jerusalem and tell the others! The Lord has risen indeed!

Narrator: They got up and returned to Jerusalem. They found the eleven and told them all that had happened.

❧ Do You Believe? ❧

by Alecia Glaize

Group 1:   One day the followers of Jesus
Were feeling quite sad and distressed.
Their longtime friend and their teacher
Had died a most terrible death.
The man they knew then as Jesus,
The Messiah, the Savior, God's Son,
No longer walked right beside them.
They feared that his message was done.

Group 2:   But Jesus had promised his followers,
On the third day, he'd be raised from the dead,
So they buried him there in the garden,
And God raised him just as God said.
When the Marys came to attend him,
The stone had been rolled away.
And an angel as bright as the lightning
Said, "He is risen on this very day."

Group 3:   Word of the miracle soon traveled.
You can't keep a good rumor down.
"Jesus is truly the Messiah!"
Was the word that went all over town.
Some women had heard Jesus talking.
With some, Jesus had shared a good meal.
At one time, he held out his hands,
And invited his disciples to feel.

Group 4:   But one of his disciples named Thomas
Said, "I just can't believe that it's true.
Jesus alive? Never happened!
Whatever you say or you do!
To convince me then, show me the nail prints,
And place my hand on his side.

53

Till then call me Thomas the doubtful.
Personally, I think that somebody lied."

Group 1:   Then something happened one evening,
As all the disciples came 'round.
And this time Thomas was with them,
But he just stood there and made not a sound.
"Peace be with you," Jesus said to them,
Then he beckoned that Thomas come near.
"Touch my hands and my side," Jesus told him.
"You have no reason to fear."

Group 2:   Thomas stood there just like a statue.
He didn't wiggle or jiggle or nod.
But these are the words that came out of his mouth,
"You are my Lord and my God."
Then Jesus smiled in a sad way,
"I know you believe 'cause you've seen.
How blessed are those among you
Who believe but have never yet seen."

Are You a Doubting Thomas?

by Denise Harris

Are you a doubting Thomas? I'll explain just what I mean—
A person who believes in things when only felt or seen.
Or do you have the faith that comes from love within your heart?
Belief in him without a doubt, from the very start!
No scientific evidence, no hands-on verification,
No facts, no forms, no proof at all, no valid confirmation.
Just the feeling deep inside that God is in control.
This knowledge comes not from the mind, but deep within the soul!

🦋 What Was Going On Up There? 🦋

by James H. Ritchie, Jr.

Jerusalem, an upper room, just before Pentecost. Several disciples are sitting around a room. Disciple 2 is looking out of a window.

Characters

Disciple 1	Disciple 2
Disciple 3	Disciple 4
Disciple 5	

Disciple 1: Get away from that window!

Disciple 2: Why? What does it matter?

Disciple 1: You know very well why.

Disciple 2: Come on! It's all a matter of time. We cannot hide from them forever. Sooner or later, they are going to figure out where we are.

Disciple 1: Let's just pray that it's later.

Disciple 3: Did you see anything down on the street?

Disciple 2: Not much. A bunch of people on their way to make their grain offerings. A couple of Roman soldiers walked by a little while ago, but they didn't even slow down.

Disciple 4: Even if they knew we were up here, I don't imagine it would make any difference to them.

Disciple 5: Why should it? As far as they're concerned, it's over. We are not news anymore.

Disciple 3: Maybe they are right.

Disciple 1: What is that supposed to mean?

Disciple 3: Maybe it is time for us to get on with our lives. We cannot spend the rest of our days hiding our faith behind locked doors.

Disciple 5: With all the time we have been spending at the Temple, how can you say that we are hiding our faith?

Disciple 3: Our faith in Jesus. That stays here.

Disciple 5: You are right. It has stayed here.

Disciple 4: I can't believe it's going to be much longer.

Disciple 5: Until what?

Disciple 4: Until we receive the power Jesus promised us.

Disciple 2: It has only been a few weeks. We haven't forgotten what he promised us, have we? "You will receive power when the Holy Spirit has come upon you..."

Disciple 4: "...and you will be my witnesses."

Disciple 1: He also told us to wait here in Jerusalem for that promise.

Disciple 5: That's the hard part.

Disciple 2: What's the hard part?

Disciple 5: The waiting.

Disciple 3: Like waiting for water to boil.

Disciple 2: Or for bread to rise.

Disciple 3: Right, like waiting for bread to rise.

Disciple 4: When we were children, it seemed to take forever.

Disciple 1: That reminds me of his parable about the leaven. The kingdom of God is like leaven, growing in almost unseen ways.

Disciple 2: That's certainly the way I grew!

Disciple 1: Unseen?

Disciple 2: No, just slowly. When I was a kid, I wondered if I was ever going to grow up. I couldn't wait to turn twelve, to be considered an adult, to be respected.

Disciple 1: That was one thing about Jesus. He respected everyone. Widows, tax collectors, lepers, women, the crippled, the blind, Samaritans...

Disciple 2: Even children!

Disciple 1: Even children.

Disciple 5: And he forgave the ones who didn't do the same.

Disciple 4: I can still hear him: "Father, forgive them, they don't know what they're doing."

Disciple 3: He welcomed people just as they were—even the sinners. Up until the very end, he kept on accepting, loving, and forgiving.

Disciple 1: Remember the time when the paralyzed man's friends tore apart the roof of the house where Jesus was?

Disciple 4: They lowered their crippled friend down into the crowd, right in front of Jesus.

Disciple 5: I can still see the shaft of sunlight beaming through the dust as they broke through, and the look on the faces of the scribes when Jesus told the man that his sins were forgiven!

Disciple 1: And the time he taught us to pray?

Disciples 2, 3, 4, & 5: Our Father, who art in heaven, hallowed be thy name. Thy kingdom come...

Disciple 2: Happy are the poor in spirit,

Disciples 3 & 4: for theirs is the kingdom of heaven.

Disciple 3: Happy are those who mourn,

Disciples 2 & 5: for they shall be comforted.

Disciple 5: Happy are the meek,

Disciples 1 & 4: for they shall inherit the earth.

Disciple 4: Bless the Lord, O my soul!

Disciples 2, 3, & 5: O Lord my God, you are very great!

Disciple 1: You make the clouds your chariot,

Disciple 2: You ride on the wings of the wind,

Disciple 3: You make the winds your messengers,

Disciple 4: Fire and flame, your ministers.

Disciple 1: What do you think it will be like when the promise comes?

Disciple 2: Will we be able to unlock the doors when we speak his name?

Disciple 5: Repentance and forgiveness of sins is to be proclaimed in his name to all nations, beginning from Jerusalem.

Disciple 3: Bless the Lord, O my soul!

Disciples 1, 2, 4 & 5: Bless the Lord, O my soul!

 Brand New!

by Karen Williams

Child One: Now, don't we all look our best?

Chorus: Brand new! Brand new!

Child One: New clothes, new shoes, and all the rest!

Chorus: Brand new! Brand new!

Child Two: But the new life Jesus gives can't be bought in the mall.

Chorus: Brand new! Brand new!

Child Two: He died and rose to save us all!

Chorus: Brand new! Brand new!

Child Three: If we are in Christ, the old is gone.

Chorus: Brand new! Brand new!

Child Three: The old is gone, the new has come.

Chorus: Brand new! Brand new!

❧ Waiting and Wondering ❧

by Virginia Kessen

Characters

Reader 1	Reader 2	Reader 3

Reader 1: Fifty days. That's how long it had been since Jesus rose from the dead. Fifty days. It wasn't long, and yet it was forever.

Reader 2: Jesus had promised to baptize the disciples with the Holy Spirit, and they were waiting. They were staying around Jerusalem waiting. Fifty days. It wasn't long, and yet it was forever.

Reader 3: "What do you think is going to happen?" they'd ask one another. "I don't know. What do you think?" So they waited. So they wondered. For fifty days, they waited and they wondered.

Reader 1: Waiting and wondering wasn't all they did. They prayed. They prayed a lot. They wanted to be ready. They wanted to be ready for—for whatever was going to happen. Fifty days. It wasn't long, and yet it was forever.

Reader 2: Then it was the Day of Pentecost, a feast day. People were in Jerusalem from all over. While the disciples were together to pray and wait, they heard a sound like the rush of a violent wind, and it filled the entire house where they were.

Reader 3: Next thing they knew, they saw tongues of fire resting on top of each one of them.

Reader 1: All the noise drew a crowd. The crowd was amazed. Even though there were people in the crowd from countries all over, they could understand what the disciples were saying.

Reader 2: "What's going on?" the people in the crowd wanted to know. "Aren't those people from Galilee? How can we understand them? We're Pathians, Medes, Elamites, and residents of Mesopotamia, Judea, Cappadocia, Pontus, and Asia; Phrygia and Pamphylia, Egypt, and Libya. We are visitors from Rome, Crete, and

Arabia. We hear them speaking about God's mighty deeds of power in our own language. What does this mean?" Others made fun of the disciples and said, "They must be drunk."

Reader 3: The disciples had waited for fifty days. Now the Holy Spirit had come. Now it was time to spread the good news about Jesus.

CPSIA information can be obtained at www.ICGtesting.com
Printed in the USA
LVOW08s0121150115

422830LV00004B/6/P